Soul Making
in the Valley of the Shadow

M000077657

Soul Making
in the Valley of the Shadow

by the Deep River Poets

Edited by Naomi Ruth Lowinsky,
Raluca Ioanid and Clare Cooper Marcus

Cover art by Kent Butzine
Design by River Sanctuary Graphic Arts

ISBN 978-1-952194-09-2
Printed in the United States of America

Additional copies available from:
www.riversanctuarypublishing.com
amazon.com

Permissions

We greatly appreciate receiving permission to reprint certain lyrics, from the following musical compositions, in two of the poems in this volume, *After the Dharma Talk* (p.80) and *Pandémie Hypnagogique* (p.91)

Werewolves of London
Words and Music by Warren Zevon, Waddy Wachtel and Leroy Marinell
Copyright © 1978 ZEVON MUSIC, LEADSHEET LAND MUSIC and TINY TUNES MUSIC. All Rights for ZEVON MUSIC administered by SONGS OF UNIVERSAL, INC. All Rights for TINY TUNES MUSIC administered by MUSIC & MEDIA INTERNATIONAL, INC.
All rights reserved. Used by Permission
Reprinted by Permission of Hal Leonard LLC and Leadsheet Land Music

Sweet Little Angel
Words and Music by B.B. King and Jules Bihari
Copyright © 1956 by Universal Music – Careers
Copyright Renewed. International Copyright Secured. All Rights Reserved
Reprinted by Permission of Hal Leonard LLC

River Sanctuary Publishing
P.O Box 1561
Felton, CA 95018
www.riversanctuarypublishing.com

*To all the poets who have visited Deep River—
from Sappho to W.S. Merwin. They have given
us the gift of their work and influenced how we
listen, how we see, how we sing our own poems.*

PROLOGUE

*Creative imagination is ...the real Ground of the psyche,
the only immediate reality. Therefore I speak of esse in
anima...(Being in the soul)*[2]

C.G. Jung

The Deep River Poets offer this collection of our poems, *Soul Making in the Valley of the Shadow*, to the Jung Institute of San Francisco, in celebration of its passage from a beloved old home to a transformative new home. This gift is an expression of deep gratitude to Extended Education, which has given Deep River support, visibility, and a sacred place to meet. We hope that sales of the book can help underwrite scholarships for those who can't afford our Public Programs.

What does it mean to Deep River that the Institute is moving from a lovely old house on a hill across from a park on Gough Street, to a beautifully renovated storefront on Mission Street? It is a move from a neighborhood of wealth and privilege, and precious little parking, to an ethnically and economically diverse part of the city, around the corner from a parking garage. It tells us that the Institute is moving out of its cloistered self-image, to a view of itself as a resource for the world—a large airy building with a low fee Psychotherapy Clinic, large and small rooms for public programs, for ARAS and for the library, which will have its own dedicated space. It shows us the Institute's wish to be accessible to people from different backgrounds and ethnicities, and, of course, people with disabilities. It opens doors to the Institute's engagement in the political and cultural life of the city and of our times, while it continues our legacy of being a treasure trove of myth, symbol, wisdom traditions and the soul work of analysis, dream work, and the expressive arts.

As Deep River's leader I must confess to powerfully conflicted feelings about our move. Like most of my colleagues my whole life as a

---

[2] *Letters I*, p.60.

i

Jungian has been housed in the Gough Street building—in the seminar room as student and as teacher, in interviews with committees deciding my Jungian fate as I applied for candidacy and was reviewed and went into "control" and was considered for certification. The building is full of the ghosts of so many who shaped my psyche, were part of the *dramatis personae* of the Institute's dramas, inspired my creativity, helped me become who I am as a person, an analyst and a poet. I even met my first important poetry mentor in the seminar room at the Institute— Diane di Prima gave a workshop and put me on her mailing list. The life of Deep River, which goes back fifteen years, has been housed in the beloved space of the library, that is until the pandemic struck and we retreated to Zoom. I find it hard to imagine leaving, though I haven't set foot in the Institute for close to a year. Where will they all go, those beloved ghosts, when we move out of our old home and into a new one?

My hope is that we will carry our ghosts as ancestors with us in our transition, that we will carry the years of Deep River meetings in the Gough St. Building library as memory and background. There is a reso- nance between the flow of Deep River's development and the Institute's move which is manifest in the poetry in this volume. The translation of one kind of home into another is symbolized by our group's move into political poetry after the 2016 election, and pandemic poetry after the assault of the coronavirus on all our lives. Like the Institute we have moved from a cloistered, inward idea of the poetic, to a more worldly, outward concern for the great issues of our time. In the new building we hope to foster mutual learning and sharing of poetry, between us and the Mission multicultural community. *Soul Making,* which began in the library of the Gough Street building, was nurtured by Extended Education, has been influenced by the spirit of our times as well as the spirit of the depths, is a manifestation of the essential role the creative arts play in the Jungian approach to healing the individual as well as the culture. May *Soul Making* serve our community as a transitional object in this transformational process.

Naomi Ruth Lowinsky

INTRODUCTION

Writing as Spiritual Practice

> *She inserts herself into everything I do. Everyday she insists*
> *on time from me, time spent listening to her. Even when*
> *I'm busy, on my way to work, or preoccupied with the news,*
> *She says: "Give me just ten minutes. That's all I ask. Sit in a*
> *chair. Take a deep breath. Take pen in your hand and write*
> *down what I say!." And you know, I always feel better after*
> *I do: more grounded, more real to myself, creative and alive.*

Naomi Ruth Lowinsky[3]

Deep River emerged fifteen years ago, out of a mountain spring in my soul, when my Muse, better known as the Sister from Below, informed me that writing poetry is my spiritual practice. Doing individual workshops did not cut it, said She, proclaiming that it was time I took my practice more seriously. She demanded a monthly poetry workshop, meeting on Second Saturdays, eight times a year. She counseled that we write under the influence of great poetry. She insisted we meet in the Institute Library, a sacred room with no doors, full of the spirits of colleagues and ancestors whose books fill the shelves. Often, a startled Jungian, expecting an empty library and easy access to the little bathroom tucked behind a nook, would tiptoe past our group. I wondered what they made of us, reading poetry aloud—Elizabeth Bishop, Galway Kinnell, Audre Lorde, or our own poems, the phrases and images of carefully crafted speech, making a soulful music in the quiet room.

How we shape shifted is a mystery, but I soon ceased to be a teacher. Instead I found myself a priestess in a coven of poets, or a minnesinger leading a band of troubadours as we wandered the many worlds of poetry. Where have we been? To name just a few of our journeys: the

---

[3] *The Sister from Below,* p.1 (Fisher King Press).

poetry of the Middle East, especially the Israeli poet Yehuda Amichai and the Palestinian poet Mahmoud Darwish; Arab and Hebrew poetry in the Golden Age of Spain when the Arabs taught the Jews that poetry could celebrate earthly life as well as God; poetry of the mystics—Rilke, Rumi, Hafiz and Rabi'a; poetry of the natural world—Wendell Berry, Gary Snyder, Pattiann Rogers; Native American poetry—Joy Harjo, Linda Hogan, N. Scott Momaday; Latinx poetry—Martín Espada, Sandra Cisneros, Rudolfo Anaya. Early on, when we dived deep into the depths of Black poetry, read Langston Hughes, Robert Hayden and Gwendolyn Brooks, listened to Roland Hayes sing spirituals, the true name of our group was revealed—Deep River.

Deep River

> *Deep River, my home is over Jordan*
> *Deep River, I want to cross over into campground*

Spiritual

The circle, like the river, is always changing. People come, people go. But a core group has emerged, that has written and studied and commented on one another's work for many years. Often in the strange way that can happen in groups, there are synchronistic resonances between people's poems. We've come to know each other's voices, each other's styles, each other's obsessions. In recent years the group has become focused on craft—listening to one another's work, commenting on it, making suggestions.

Since the trauma of the 2016 election and the catastrophic times that have followed, Deep River has become a sacred river we wash ourselves in, as the Hindus do in Ganga Ma—Mother Ganges—to cleanse our souls and heal our broken hearts. We've studied the poetry of witness and of engagement, written under the influence of poets whose work flows between the political and the spiritual—Federico García Lorca, Pablo Neruda, Robert Bly, Carolyn Forché, Lucille Clifton, Agha Shahid Ali, Judy Grahn, W.S. Merwin. Their writings are at once a stimulus for our own work, and a balm for our wounded spirits. They help us cross over from the realm of conscious life to the realm of the unconscious, from the land of the living to the land of the dead. We gather at the river to follow the flow of our poems; they take us to unexpected places, show us the unexpected—the tree of life around a bend in the river, its roots deep in the earth.

Rivers of Blood

> *Someone asked me what I thought about world events in the near future. I said that I had no thoughts, but saw blood, rivers of blood.*

C.G. Jung[4]

Though Deep River has never been overtly Jungian, Jung is the big fish who swims in our depths. In our recent cataclysmic times, I've been haunted by the visions Jung experienced over a hundred years ago—rivers of blood, hordes of the dead. These led to his creation of *The Red Book*—the quintessential work of "Soul Making in the Valley of the Shadow." In it he recorded his visions, his visitations by inner figures, his conversations with them. The book also contains his powerful paintings of archetypal images.

Unbeknownst to Jung, in 1913, he was foreseeing a catastrophe—the gathering insanity which would become World War I was seeping into his psyche. He feared he was suffering a breakdown. When the First World War broke out, he actually felt relieved—understanding that his visions were not about himself personally, but about the approaching collective calamity. In the Introduction to *The Red Book* Sonu Shamdasani describes the central theme:

> how Jung regains his Soul and overcomes the
> contemporary malaise of spiritual alienation...The
> task of individuation lay in establishing a dialogue
> with the fantasy figures—or contents of the collective
> unconscious—hence recovering the value of the mythpoeic

---

[4] *The Red Book*, p. 199 (W.W. Norton and Company).

imagination…and …reconciling the spirit of the time with the spirit of the depths.[5]

The Red Book was the vessel in which Jung gathered his splintered psyche.

On Making Poems and Soul

> *I am the tree of life whose roots go down into childhood, into the realm of the ancestors, into the dream world, into the myths that shape you, into the secret power of the very language you use…*
>
> *When you are moved, when affect and image come together, there I am. When you breathe deeply, and know what you are feeling, there I am. When a fragment of a dream comes back and invades your daylight mind, there I am… I am the poet in you, your Sister from Below, the voice of what is deep in you, wild in you, erotic in you.*
>
> Naomi Ruth Lowinsky[6]

In our own awful times, the safe world that those of us with privilege have taken for granted has been severely shaken. We are terrorized by extreme weather—heat waves, hurricanes, flooding, tornadoes and wildfires, by the extinction of species, by a corrupt, incompetent, authoritarian and rabble-rousing president. Our ghosts claw their way out of our dark closets, cobwebbed attics, musty basements, like the "thronging dead of human history, the ghostly procession of the past"[7] which haunted Jung over a hundred years ago. They threaten us with what our ancestors most feared—loss of our homes and homeland, famine, drought, and persecution. In the midst of all this comes the pandemic and soon after the Black Lives Matter protests all over our country and the world.

---

[6] *The Sister from Below*, pp. 7-8.
[7] *The Red Book*, p. 296.

We've retreated to our individual homes, like cloistered contemplatives in the Dark Ages. Deep River has retreated to Zoom. The Unknown roils around us, as does hope—the possibility of change, of winning an election, of making a vaccine, of creating a more egalitarian society. In Deep River we found ourselves writing pandemic poems. Someone suggested we publish a collection of them. Someone else said, let's make it broader, more inclusive of our writings. And so it was that we began gathering this harvest of our years together.

You may ask, what can poetry possibly do when our lives are stripped down to the bone, when we must wear masks to go out in public, when we depend on "essential workers"—often the poor and people of color—to bring us our food and take care of the outer world, where they are at risk while we are protected. What is poetry's role?

To make a poem requires seeking the right words, images, musical rhythms, to voice the unbearable, say the unsayable, illuminate the numinous—whether it be an awe inspiring or terrifying experience from childhood, the joys or agonies of love and family, the terrors of climate change, a chaotic president, systemic racism or an invisible killer. Making a poem doesn't change what happens but it shifts our relationship to it. The Muse is the voice of the soul, speaking in language that blends reason and mystery, She makes meaning out of the incomprehensible. In *The Red Book* Jung has given us a luminous model of how the creative imagination can transform the unbearable and the unfathomable. Writing and painting in dialogue with the unconscious was his spiritual practice. He had to confront his shadow, honor the dead, find his roots in the earth, his passion for life, and most importantly he had to submit to the demands of his soul. It was through that process of dialogue with his inner figures that the wisdom which became his psychology was revealed to him. Though Jung vigorously denied being an artist, *The Red Book* proves him wrong. In the making of it, Jung has shown us our path. That is why I've chosen epigraphs from *The Red Book,* to divide the sections of poetry in this anthology, because Jung's way is, essentially, Deep River's way.

Section I: We face our collective and personal shadow.

Section II: We make contact with the dead.

Section III: We encounter our Tree of Life.

Section IV: Symbols come to us, unbidden, open new rooms.

Section V: In the company of our souls, we find Our Way.

>In Jung's words:
>Great is the power of the way. In it Heaven and Hell grow together, and in it the power of the Below and the power of the Above unite. The nature of the way is magical...[8]

Our way is the way of the poet, who knows that poems have lives of their own. Poems need us, their poets, to listen to them, see them, feel them, wrestle with them until their hidden natures emerge. In return they reflect us, revise us, refine us, play us like musical instruments; they shape shift our stories and light up dim corners of our souls. The craft of making a poem becomes a craft—a vessel—for knowing ourselves and our world.

Naomi Ruth Lowinsky

---

[8] *The Red Book,* p. 308.

Contents

Contents, cont.

III

Contents, cont.

Contents, cont.

I believe in the poetry of the dreamtime. I believe it is essential that our poetry reach back to the roots of human consciousness and retrieve our collective soul. I believe poetry is one way we bring ourselves back into relation with the moon, animals, plants, and ancestors.[1]

Naomi Ruth Lowinsky

[1] from "The Muse of the Moon," in *The Dream and Its Amplification* edited by Erel Shalit and Nancy Swift Furlotti, p. 92 (Fisher King Press).

Winnowing Basket

The heart is a vessel of wheat
I am separating slowly
It's a task that was written by the stars
The work spans factories, coal mines,
kitchens, libraries, classrooms,
airports, trains, coffee shops and mountain trails

For centuries, I have been polishing the mirror
The gift I was given: a winnowing basket

Separate grain by grain,
thought by thought
step by step
line by line
breath by breath

sand from the ocean
joining from distance
silence from word
sight from vision
life from death

Daniela Kantorová

I

And thus I went out in that night (it was the second night of the year 1914), and anxious expectation filled me… The path was wide and what was to come was awful. It was the enormous dying, a sea of blood…

As darkness seized the world, the terrible war arose and the darkness destroyed the light of the world… And so we had to taste hell…

C.G. Jung[9]

---

[9] *The Red Book*, p. 274.

Why Poetry?

The 2016 U.S. presidential election revealed this country's steady descent into the valley of its historically unrecognized shadow. This election placed a psychologically unfit, misogynistic, racist man in the seat of a juggernaut set on an implosion course: police brutality captured in a nine–minute recording, children torn from their parents and kept in cages; and even white people taking to the streets to proclaim Black Lives Matter during this life-taking pandemic. These are just a few of the many events shaking the foundational beliefs of the great American experiment. Truths once declared to be self-evident now trampled and discarded in exchange for power and profit.

During this same time period I have experienced the deaths of family members and long–time friends as well the birth of a grandchild. How does one hold the pain, anger and disbelief of the injustices in this country, the grief that accompanies death as well as the joys of life? The practice of writing a personal record of witness through poetry is my way. To condense the felt experiences, unapologetically affirm what I see as true, provoke inquiry, promote reflection and reveal the sacred in the mundane are the goals I aspire to achieve. It is my wish that my poems weave a medicine basket to hold the unbearable, the miraculous and even the humorous in service of the soul.

Anita Cadena Sánchez

Will This Ever End

History has many cunning passages, contrived corridors
And issues, deceives with whispering ambitions,
Guides us by vanities.

T.S. Eliot [10]

January 20, 2017
Without notice the White House grows whiter yet
invisible swastikas slide off the frozen walls

Stealthy they glide along marble floors
Without notice they slip beneath guarded doors

Without sound they pass protestors in the streets
Without stopping they slither once more into the Mind of Time

With malice towards most and charity for the powerful few
With justice and peace for some

May 25, 2020
Shadows emerge from sliding doors
a chain of events unbroken

We stand on uncertain ground
Mind grips tight but the brain wants to disbelieve

what the eyes see and the ears hear
The pit of the stomach knows fear

My fingers grip the inkless pen
Only rooted beliefs can explain such brutality

---

[10] from "Gerontion" *T.S. Eliot: The Complete Poems and Plays,* p. 22
(Harcourt, Brace and World).

Around the world they see the bad & ugly
in America—captured on the screen

The president conflates
Black Lives Matter with hate

So I draw in breath to settle and center
Yes, I can breath but I witness who can't

Another black man dies
again   and again   and again

                                        Anita Cadena Sánchez

In the Soup

I am walking through soup
a thick heavy soup that slows
me down makes it hard to see

I don't know what kind of soup it is

Don't know if the soup is hot
or my soul is burning

Don't know if I'm lost
or don't care where I am

Don't know if I'm crying
or singing

Don't know if I'm ready to die
or to live at last in aliveness

Don't know what I'll do
without you

Kent Ward Butzine

then & now

in that sliver of time
the Before   the Now

some people scrambled for rolls and rolls of toilet paper
others bought a gazillion gallons of bottled water

I opted for cash on hand, gas in the tank and
a pantry brimming with a rainbow of dried beans
but overnight cash was no longer king
and no place felt safer than home

we didn't realize then what we would miss most
but you cannot store "things" which cannot be bought

those "things" I freely dispensed without much concern
and with even lesser thought

before March 17th when the governor declared
Bay Area citizens—you must shelter–in–place
you and I were free to touch to hug to hold

now   we quarantine that kiss and hold off on hugs
we wash our hands & wear our masks
6 feet apart is how we stand to show our love

still the body aches
for tender   touch

Anita Cadena Sánchez

The Three Minute Woman

From my 10th floor apartment in West Tower
I see a man washing his shirt in the plaza fountain below
not a public place even though people
once walked through the plaza to the now shuttered cinema
and sat on the benches to eat lunch
and read newspapers from the bookstore now closed
and drink wine at the Flower Box bar that still sells a few flowers but
is now shut

The man runs away leaving his black shirt in the cold water
after he sees Lance the security guard
who picks up the wet shirt with his ungloved hand
throws it in the trash beside the ATM
the fountain is not a laundry.

Riding the elevator down from West Tower
we stop on the 7th floor where
a woman enters making it impossible
to keep the 6 ft distance
to stop the spread of a deadly virus
There are already 3 in the elevator
She insists it is her right to ride down with us
because she had to wait
3 minutes
for the other elevator
that must be out of order.

A woman stands on a ramp at the entrance to the West Tower
twisting a tree limb that stretches itself helplessly into her space
while she talks on her cell phone about her stocks
now crashed
She shakes the trembling limb like it was a money tree.

When I return to the 10th floor
to be walled in once more
I take the other elevator
the one the 3 minute woman said wasn't working
She must not have understood there is a fast moving
virus going around
spread by droplets that linger
in the air of slow elevators.

Best each one rides alone.
Wait patiently for the world to come back to you
When it will.

Virginia Lee Chen

Macy's, Late Winter

With rubber gloves
I paw through last season's gym wear
push one item against the other
inside their wobbly steel racks.

A saddle of sweatpants
across my arm, I head
to the dressing room—Closed.
I eye a human huddle:
one employee
wearing a metallic
plum rayon sweater—
the saleslady who has
bagged my bras
and briefs for twenty years.
I overhear her:
How long will the store stay closed?
And will they pay us?

The "Shelter–in–Place" order
begins at midnight
and I am one of three customers
on the 4th floor. I drop my face mask
to greet the young Eritrean couple
in a sea of Puma, Nike,
& Adidas running suits
who tell me: *Target ran out*
of toilet paper yesterday.

I begin to worry about Macy's
I begin to worry about Macy employees
I begin to worry about downtown.

Hitting the bricks, my old boss
Pell, called it. Such a dignified butch
short grey cornrows, violet eyes,
a pile of shiny silver bangles
across her wrists. On her day off—
in leather shoes with steel heels—
she'd strike the brick
paths of Market Street,
O'Farrell, Maiden Lane—
took freedom seriously.

My sales lady lifts her eyeglasses
from a nylon string around her neck,
scans my sweatpants. Our eyes
meet in a cauldron about to boil.
On the escalator ride down
workers zigzag their attention
from phones to one last look
at manikins wearing
Spring's new colors:
Marine Blue, Harbor Mist, Lime Punch.

Connie Hills

Target, I Love You

Hungrily, I finger piles of bright tank tops, fluorescent lacy bras,
polka dot socks
all sweat shop mass–produced, unsustainable, unfairly traded.
I don't care.
I want to heap my cart, my life,
my intestines to the brim
with multi-colored softness.

Each synthetic fiber of these Dora the Explorer rainbow underwear
proof of somewhere's destruction
someone's oppression.

Cargo ships heave
detritus of consumption
to and fro from China.
Rubber duckies, mismatched sneakers and L.E.D. key chains are lost
in transit.
Wayward plastic forms new archipelagos.

Our hunger cannot be sated.

Raluca Ioanid

Precipice

A steep decline in the value of your investments
Is called
A waterfall drop

What happens below
In the green river
Feeding the dark lake
To the underworld
Where the dead have gone
And the mortals
  In their grief
  Go down
  Hoping to bring their loved ones back
  Or failing that
  Hoping to stay down forever
  In that place where nothing can fall

Virginia Lee Chen

Blurdays

every day rolls into
the next without distinction

an exit–less revolving door
every 24 hours so like the previous 24

without the busy calendar to color
in the hours with engagements, appointments and events

each day becomes a carbon copy
of the day before

caught in a hallway of facing mirrors
yesterday and today endlessly replicating
into an almost identical tomorrow

during these daunting days
we wonder how many more can we endure

we worry we wait while
sheltering restlessly in the same place

stunned and suspended in this indeterminate state
caught in the world's sudden pause

Anita Cadena Sánchez

With My Pink Pussy Hat On

The man who thinks he is
                my president
conferred with the press today
all these pigeons
flapping and cooing
at the elephant trumpeting
so stupidly we might laugh,
but   he's   not   kidding.

Stark afraid,
intestines twisting,
                I wish
I could throw up
what I cannot swallow.

How will we open our hearts
                to each other
in a country where half the voters are in love
with their hating

of people like me: like for instance:
                women they can't own, or men who can
love other men,
                or those who belong to other cultures
                    part of Humanity's far flung treasure,

or the words at the feet that Liberty
stands upon.
How can we survive
in a land where immigrant
has become an insult?

Who will help the young women
denied birth control,
or give them gentle treatment for infections
gifted to them by young men
who claim to love them.

What about our artists? Are they ghosts
on a burning ship?

As I drive by cliffs and surf,
                    windows open
where the first wild iris
ruffles in a sweet breeze

an ugly voice, rude,
smug, spits from the radio
lying. Obviously. Brutality unveiled:
No pretense. No bother:
If you want to feel bigger,
you can always make someone else
feel small.

When greed is unbridled
and hatred, fashionable,
slave labor an industry,
and a maddened demagogue with a fist
full of Tomahawks controls
our radio
activity

Are we all condemned
to live in illusion
and call it
privilege?

Much as I love my pink pussy hat,
I fear it can't protect me from this
elephantine Juggernaut,
All of us,
crushed.

Dossie Easton

Medicine Wheel

1.

Each April   you lose sight of the mountain
as green leaves take over the trees
You've been here before   and yet

Have you ever been round   such a wheel   of changes?
This time last year   you were gripped
by that agonized hip   Pain

was your shepherd   your cane   your walker
in the land   of the invalid   in the time
of medical marijuana   in the season of the Surgery

Waiting Room   You sat   among the resigned   the terrified
On the silent TV   the Man made of Greed   and his Handmaiden
descended the golden escalator

Hecate of the Crossroads   What do you see?

2.

This spring   it keeps raining   long past
the equinox   after how many seasons
of drought?   Your scar is healing

On a day blessed by sun   you and your Dan walk round
the reservoir   all the long   lovely   up and down of it
drinking in smells and bird sightings

while the Wild Man of Mar-a-Lago
and the Fat Boy of Pyongyang
square off   with missiles…

This is the spring Erdogan   steals Turkey
Maduro   sacks Venezuela   Le Pen looms
over Pax Europa   Putin's unmasked   as puppeteer

Kali   Lend us your Axe

3.
You are a woman regaining your stride
You take to the streets   as though
the wheel turned back   to 1968

The Woman's March
The "Show Us Your Taxes March"
The March for Science   on Earth Day

The Stand Off at Standing Rock
The Elders say   Water is Life
Just ask the People of Flint

Just ask the People of Nogales   what a wall will do
to the Rio Grande   its flood plains   its families
its Mexican Gray Wolf

Blessed are they who wash the feet of the stranger

4.
This is the year you let go   the long horizon
At one   and at odds
in peace   and in pieces

astride Lady Fortuna's   wild wheel
in the grip   of the Man made of Greed
the danger that lives   in his eyes

Whomever he strikes   he strikes
in your name   Whoever strikes back
strikes you   and your sweet   beloveds

Destiny is a frayed rope
holding onto the boat
as seas rise...

Mother of Changes   hold on to us

Naomi Ruth Lowinsky

Dead Pheasants

This time I saw them and remembered

"Three pounds fifty a brace"
the sign said above the box of
dead pheasants
eyes clouded milky cumulus
feathers berry–red and green
like winter ivy fading to
angry bruising of betrayal

I remember you strutting like
jeweled princes in the sunlit fields
of childhood
I remember proud tails
regal collars
raucous cries when danger
lurked

I remember wallowing in the cooling
waters of a brook we thought of as
the Nile
climbing a beech tree in a wind
that tempest–tossed our bodies
till we felt sick with ecstasy

Mornings full of horses' hoofs
on cobbles
swallows in black arrow
squadrons diving low over piles of
steaming dung
evenings full of dark–bodied planes
returning from missions dropping
death

The pheasants lie close
as lovers
breast upon breast
as in the aching scar of Babi Yar
where bodies pressed
bone upon bone
in the unfamiliar intimacy of
death

Clare Cooper Marcus

Near Midnight

to Else Lasker-Schüler[11]

She had to do it—
She had no idea why—
But when near midnight she heard screams,
                    she broke his neck.

Silence spread everywhere. Sprang
from her hands to the small limp rabbit.
To the hunter whose .22 and spotlight were
                    not enough.

Silence seeped everywhere. Into everything.
Into the frozen bloodied ground.
And then lay over our mouths.

Sheila deShields

---

[11] Else Lasker-Schüler was a German-Jewish poet, associated with
Expressionism, who fled Nazi Germany in the early 1930s and made
her home in Jerusalem.

Ashes

San Francisco, February, 2020

"Tourists still come here"
to the burnt out land
Do they buy bottled water?
The earth shakes a little
They are well groomed
What sights are on their lists,
and do they see the ghosts?

A man in rags on a corner is laughing out loud
Another is walking barefoot wrapped in a thick, dirty blanket
I remember a resort in Goa
with shacks attached to its walls
I was a tourist then, I had fun

Flights are grounded
Flights are diverted to military bases
Flights are shot down
"Remember flight, the bird is mortal"
I remember
My heart is spilling over with ashes

I remember trips to Metreon during the early days
New in California.
Not knowing the name of Idriss Stelley[12]

Now I remember
Jessica Nelson
Mario Woods
Kenny Harding
Amilcar Perez Lopez
Luis Gongora Pat

Alex Nieto
O'Shaine Evans
Darnell Benson
Derrick Gaines

But tourists still come here
the skyline grows
I try to remember my name
Who am I and why am I here
a friend told me, not to forget
Tourists still come here
The food is good

Daniela Kantorová

---

[12] Idriss Stelley was killed by SFPD in 2003, Kenneth Harding Jr. was killed by SFPD in 2011, Derrick Gaines was killed by South San Francisco police in 2012, Alex Nieto was killed by SFPD in 2014, O'Shaine Evans was killed by SFPD in 2014, Amilcar Perez Lopez was killed by SFPD in 2015, Darnell Benson was killed by sheriff deputies in San Francisco County Jail, in 2015, Mario Woods was killed by SFPD in 2015, Luis Gongora Pat was killed by SFPD in 2016, Jessica Nelson was killed by SFPD in 2016.

Sibyl

The Sibyl inhales deeply
The vapors from the fire below
She is no longer herself
She from a respectable family
She who is reliably self–possessed
Is unhinged by the smell of death

The odors waft from underneath
The fragrance of a vague melody
Swirls before her
She murmurs a few slanted comments
Her voice hoarse from Sulphur
She is weak from what she sees

Wants to go back to imagining
A lover waiting for her on the other side
If only she could let go of her beliefs that
What has come before her is real
The visionary longs for the return of dreams
To lose herself once more in those magical images

Promising a life fulfilled by words
Love from one who imagines her
Soft deceits are prophecies
for the days of wholeness
That can never be

Virginia Lee Chen

II

Take pains to waken the dead…

*I see behind you, behind the mirror of your eyes,
the crush of dangerous shadows, the dead, who look
greedily through the empty sockets of your eyes, who
moan and hope to gather up through you all the
loose ends of the ages, which sigh in them.*

C.G. Jung[13]

---

[13] *The Red Book*, p. 244, 296.

In Awful Times

I wake in the night to the sound of ominous growling from the heavens. Is it war planes? Is it a massive explosion like the one that shattered Beirut? We are in the midst of a red flag heat wave. Even in the night it's unbearably hot. Have the gods gone crazy? Are they throwing thunder and lightning at us in the middle of a pandemic, in fire season, in August, in California, where we never have summer storms?

The ominous growl keeps repeating its menace. I get the message—it's angry, and it's bigger than we are—we mortals. I sense that I am hearing the uprising fury of the dead, those who died unable to breathe, with a policeman's knee on their neck, or an invisible power destroying their lungs. I hear them thundering their losses, wailing about their beloveds, who could not touch them, hold them, kiss them goodbye. Their sorrow howls in me and I realize, as horrifying as their growing numbers are, I haven't wept for them, I haven't stomped my feet on the ground, keened, poured ashes over my head, torn my clothes.

Strange, since I am one who lives with my dead—the many kin who died in the Shoah, my Oma's children who died too young—they're in my writings, in my poems, in Oma's paintings all over my house. But this catastrophe under the surface of our awful times, this hell realm where people must die alone, traps the dead in some weird virtual reality, split off from our human touch. We need to learn Jung's approach to the dead: "The spirits of those who die before their time will live, for the sake of our present incompleteness, in dark hordes in the rafters of our houses and besiege our ears with urgent laments, until we grant them redemption…"[14]

The dead are our past and our future, our roots in the millennia, the Deep River of continuity that nourishes our souls and feeds our poetry. In awful times especially, we owe the dead our poems, and our awe. Remember the conflicted meanings of "awe"—dread, reverence, wonder.

Naomi Ruth Lowinsky

---

[14] *The Red Book*, p. 297.

Why Am I Here?
Le Palais de Papes, Avignon, August 2018

because this is the walled city   of the broken bridge
because I have been to the cave   seen the handprint
                    of our ancestor   waving   waving
                                        in red ochre
because mother is dead
and I need a tincture   of my European essence
because I sit in a circle of strangers   we all speak alchemy
                                some of us speak Motherline

because the *mistral* blows fierce   all over Provence
                    will fling you down   knock you up
                                        against the walls
because the Inquisition lasted five hundred years
because no one gets out of here alive
because we understand   this pompous pile of popery
                                        is Bluebeard's castle
because they herded up my ancestors   drove them into the fire
because the right wing is rising in the West   rules the East
because the plane trees have lost their bark
                                        because of the drought
because there is no rescue   from overwhelm
        will Europa be savaged again
        like the blue spangled manikin   in the garden
                            without hands   without feet?

because we are all in the same boat
        all immigrants from Africa
        all fleeing some ancient terror
        all children of the children of the children

of the grandmothers who knew   baking bread
is the sacred precinct of the women   requires silence
                                       no man dare intrude

because we are sitting on linens   our mothers' mothers embroidered
        in the graveyards of Eastern Europe   listening
                                       to their bones   their blood

because I belong to the grief   and the terrible stories
because I have been to the cave   and seen   the Paleolithic mare
                           from when poetry began
                           loping back into the dark

                                       Naomi Ruth Lowinsky

Moon

The sonographer's magic wand
pokes and prods my recesses,
a glowing screen
illuminates the apparatus of creation.

Relief.
Here, the uterus.
There, the swirling orbs of ovaries
that came into this life containing all their eggs.

Inside my grandmother's ancestral womb,
lived both her daughters and the oocytes of future grandchildren,
just as inside of me dwells the possibility of new lives,
lives that will outlast me.

Months ago I found myself in a similar dark room,
holding my mother's frightened leg,
the only part of her that I could reach,
soothing, as best I could,
as the sonographer waved her jelly-covered wand
across the milk white of my mother's breasts.

I hadn't seen my mother's naked body in decades,
the rosiness of her flesh startled me.
The inside of her breasts glowed on the ultrasound screen,
transformed into an undulating lunar landscape.

I clung to her as though I
could keep her here,
protect her from that lawless, roadless entropy
that threatens to overtake her cells.

The sonographer and I peered anxiously into the moon-like
image.

There, I imagined the death that will one day take her,
and our life together rewound to the beginning,
her womb a dark laboratory of creation,
my violent arrival,
her milk nourishing me.

It is written.
Inside of us,
the lives we can create and sustain with our bodies
and the cells that will unravel our existence.

Raluca Ioanid

Dream Kitchen

I dream I want to ask you
Are you still alive?
I wake up remembering you died

I dream I am cooking 3 artichokes
In an old Chinese wok with the lid on
I leave the room for a moment

The sound of an explosion
Goes through my body
A fatal thought

I left you unattended

I rush into the kitchen
Expecting to see bits of pale green
On the floor   on the walls

All is quiet
Except for the soft sound of boiling water
I slowly lift the lid

You are whole
Serenely waiting
Unbroken intact

You trust
I will know
The right time

To take you out
When the rawness
Has gone away

Virginia Lee Chen

Threshold

After I die I will sit perched atop a dilapidated Victorian
 on an East Oakland hill
surrounded by bushes of roses that have become trees
the abundance of blossoms my treasure

Perhaps reminiscing how I walked one early grey afternoon in May
in drizzling rain on a quiet residential street with soothing trees

Looking at withering roses,
As if counting the wilting petals
Breathing in, I'm alone
Breathing out, I'm not alone
Or somewhere in-between
Crossing the street
Crossing the border
Oakland the *Barzakh*[15] city
training ground
In between heaven and hell
at the rose scented Threshold
the soft breeze whispers
you're not alone
you have no choice in that

Daniela Kantorová

---

[15] *Barzakh* (from Arabic and Persian) means partition. Mentioned in the Quran, Surah XXIII, verse 100, it describes a state between death and resurrection.

September Morning

The sweet smell of lung cancer
lingers in the room
where my sister died.

She said she had no one
no child
no husband
not even a cat to keep her warm.

But her sister took care of her
during those months the brain declined
when tumors lived inside her mind
until she found her on the bed
one September morning
dead.

At once the sister saw
death doesn't symbolize anything
there's nothing underneath.

And what about love?
Love doesn't stand for anything either
Love stands for itself alone.

Virginia Lee Chen

heartache

sorrow is your other name
who am I now
but a motherless woman
child
so much lost
in the sea of forgotten memories
who was I to know
what cannot be known
until the casket closed

Anita Cadena Sánchez

Funeral Cot

I'm rocking a funeral cot
The fire is burning
The fire shall not eat my body
I shall eat the fire
In fire I remain cold
I'm singing a lullaby
to the rhythm of bones
cracking in the fire
There is a baby in the funeral cot
I feel the wind
I see a grove of silver birch on the horizon
Patches of wild thyme
Two pines in the field
My fertility is meant for dirt
for the flowing river
for the spider web of stars
Breathe me
Breathe my dust
as I sit by the fire
I absorb the sun in my bones
I wait for the lamp to break
I wait for the release of light

Daniela Kantorová

Time to Come

Oh, mother! He was my own, own brother.
Theodore Van Gogh

If you visit Van Gogh's grave
go after the gust of summer.
When gaunt air fills your lungs.
When the patisserie pulses with locals
lined up for Pan au Chocolat,
Framboise Shortbread,
Chaussons Aux Pommes,
Quiche aux Champignon.

Go when aspen leaves fall
from the height of autumn
spilling pools of yellow
to the cobblestone below.
And leaf blowers—
men wrapped in wool
pants and crimson scarves—
noise their way up
the gutted gravel hill of Auvers
its stone wall enclosing
a grey sea of tombs.

When rain clouds hover
over the famed wheat fields
floating into eternity.
The quaintness of the place
so placid you imagine
standing at Vincent's burial
that July midi
surrounded by lemon sunflowers,
battered dahlias

Hallelujahs oozing
from their thousands of
amber throats.

Side by side tombstones:
a great artist, his beloved brother
beneath a blanket of ivy
at the world's vast edge
under a swirling blue sky.

Connie Hills

A Villanelle for My Father

As you lay dying
I didn't ask you questions about your life
Questions to trigger conversation
Questions inviting you to talk.

I didn't ask you about your life
The bicycle tour of central France
Questions inviting you to talk
A woman named Zita you loved and left.

With Bertie Dale, your childhood friend
On bicycles in a sepia print
A woman named Zita you loved and left
Because your mother didn't approve.

On bicycles in a sepia print
Two young men, now gone, now gone
Because your mother didn't approve
What of the women in Italy?

Two young men, now gone, now gone.
Life and love both fleeting fast
What of the women in Italy?
You loved them too and had to leave.

Life and love both fleeting fast
You loved us and left for the war
You loved them and had to leave
Was there a child you left behind?

You loved us and left for the war
Across the seas in a foreign land
Was there a child you left behind?
Or were there two—one here, one there?

Across the seas in a foreign land
Questions to trigger conversation
Were there two—one here, one there?
Questions inviting you to talk
    As you lay dying.

                Clare Cooper Marcus

How To Pack a Sandwich

Place the sandwich in the middle
of a square piece of wax paper.
Pull up two sides around
the hull of the sandwich.
Pinch and fold. Rotate.
Twist-tie a knot on top
till it's sealed for travel.

Remember to smell
the tang of the tomato
the Jarlsberg's salty brine
smoke of the ham.
Remember your ancestors—
huddled in the Lyngdal farmhouse
before boarding the ship to America.
How they placed these
packets of nourishment
deep in their rucksacks
beside the dented thermos
of hot coffee sweetened
with fresh cow's milk.

How folding and packing sandwiches—
the Norwegian way—
lies somewhere in your DNA.
How you will die like this—
You are not afraid of the sea.

Connie Hills

45

Bucharest 1958 Sestina

History churns inside the family of ghosts,
we cannot forget,
unmoored by our
ancestral loss,
unravelling backwards from a nightmare–dream
we search eternally for Anita and Paul, our disappeared parents.

The abduction of these beloved parents
propelled us into the land of hungry ghosts.
Here, we dream
and struggle to forget.
We are punctured by memory holes of loss,
our insides leaking out, hour by hour.

Dutifully we sleepwalk our
hollow impersonations of how adults and parents
should be. Our glacier of loss
has frozen us into child ghosts
forever trapped in the night the secret police came. Forget
we cannot, Anita and Paul are ever present in the worlds of our
dreams.

What might we dream
if the hours
and years allowed a glossy patina of forgetting
to engulf the ragged edges of our parent–less
grief? What new ghosts
might inhabit our loss?

Is there any light inside this loss?
Do the holes inside us make us dream
bigger? Speaking to us from the land of the ghosts,

to this new generation, perhaps our
vanished grandparents
have impelled us to live greatly, in the shadow of what we cannot
forget.

In our pact never to forget,
the momentum of loss
is greater. Have our night–vanishing grandparents
opened the door for dreams
and days and meals and adventures sweetened by our
kinship to this family of ghosts?

We cannot forget, but in our dreams
there is an alchemy of loss in which the heat and pressure of our
lost grandparents transmutes us from ghosts into butterflies.

Raluca Ioanid

Medicine Basket
For adult children made orphans during this pandemic

In that lost space
sucking you out of
your center of certainty

your mind now mindless
a torrent of tears stream from
your crows' feet into the crevices
of your laugh lines

your nose drips sorrow
your parched mouth murmurs prayers
your heart though shattered beats

so it is
when that final breath
of the surviving spouse of that couple
you knew as your parents
returns from where it came

you
stand
alone

no mother, no father
to console you
to advise or scold you

to retell family stories
of their own journeys

made before you were born

slowly let your heart mend
gently pull yourself together

recognize your place on the
precipice of time

you are the last living generation
of the six that went before you

passing that invisible medicine basket[16]
from one generation to the next

it's your turn to gather up
your scattered wisdom

those whisperings you heard
when at the water's edge or under trees

that knot in your stomach that refused to
budge until you summoned the courage to act

the dismantling of barbed wire guarding
your heart until you forgave yourself

Remember
the next six generations depend on you.

Anita Cadena Sánchez

---

[15] This poem borrows from the Haudenosaunee (Iroquois) philosophy that advocates remembering how today's decisions and actions echo into the future, and specifically, how they will impact the next seven generations. The poet is asking readers to recognize their place as elders, recall the wisdom passed on to them, and to gather their insights to be placed in a metaphorical medicine basket to be carried forward.

Civic Center

I hear the beep of trucks
Moving backwards
Sporadic car alarms
Screech of metal

I breathe in and out

An ambulance squeals
Joined by a police car siren
The breath of their engines
Project harsh sounds
Into my undefended ears

I open my eyes

Looking down from my 10th story apartment window
A barefoot man wearing a black tee shirt and shorts
Leaps and screams on the street corner
He pays no attention to the street lights
Red or Green

He vanishes

Yesterday was the third anniversary
Of my grandchild's violent death
Killed by a car in front of his school
Blood running down the street
Along with his astonished classmates
Silence

I hear the soft snap snap
Of a hummingbird wing
Among the purple fuchsias
On my balcony

I turn to look as it flies away

                    Virginia Lee Chen

Anne Frank's Tree

Whirring blades
scatter sawdust like white–weeping stars
onto the courtyard sky.
There was a window where she watched

                                                  eye of hope

small opening to sailing galaxies
fussing flocks of starlings
on darkening eaves.

In spring, chestnut flowers
like ghostly candelabra
lit her days, as they did mine
not much distance west, across
the channel.
White and pink flowers in April
chestnuts in October
round brown glossy like silk
we strung them, hung them
on knotted twine playing conkers
till someone was declared
the champion.

For her, the tree beyond her grasp
stood achingly alive, dear daily reminder
of leaf–birth,
                 leaf fall,
season's sweet swing
weather's wanderlust
clouds cleaving the sky
cirrus   cumulus   stratus

divine draperies
obliterating darkening rumors of
yellow stars
    feared betrayals
        cattle cars.

Sixty years on
they say the tree is dying
impossible to save.
They say the workmen hired
to bring it down were
weeping.

                Clare Cooper Marcus

Song of the Vulture

The ragpickers have abandoned
    the battlefield, dust
has come to settle like blankets
     over the naked dead.

Soon the air will be perfumed
with the tangible honey
    of blossoming flesh.
Skin sloughs, muscles
      soften like peaches in the sun.

Flies build nests in eyes that watched,
Crows dispatch lips and noses,
    leave the fallen faceless.
The defeated do not bury their dead;
they are lost to immortality.

I keep vigil
     on the timeless updraft,
       and wait for them to ripen.
When the sweetness rises on the wind
and the spoils of war spill out shining
        from the guts split open,

I and my sisters will honor their flesh
offer them up to their rightful cause:
strip them down to meat and bones
and scatter their composition
to feed the earth
      that saw them born.

Dossie Easton

The Day (in America) I Didn't Know My Guru Died

Just past dusk in this lush
jungle of South India
(8,000 miles from home)
I stand naked in a hotel shower
my feet gripping its wet
bright white glass tiles.
Don't slip,
I tell myself as I
rinse the surrealism
off this winter day:
a loop de loop bus ride
along vertiginous roads
green petticoats of tea bushes
covering volcanic earth;
our tour guide pouring
Old Monk rum into paper
cups—sipping the elixir
like an eastern Absinthe;
kaleidoscopic sunclouds
flickering shadows over
a 3–hour locomotive chug
through ten inky tunnels
dug into blue mountains;
our knee–to–knee boxcar
besieged by wild vines
their purple wispy tails—
sticky & pungent —spilling
in over the jammed-open
metal window, spirits
entering me in the thick air.

Connie Hills

III

*I ate the earth and I drank the sun and I became a
greening tree that stands alone and grows.*

C.G. Jung[17]

---

[17] *The Red Book,* p. 273.

Two Saturdays

I saw the seminar advertised somewhere on campus: "Object– emotion relations." I thought this might be interesting. My whole career had focused on raising the consciousness of architecture students (and the architecture profession) on understanding the psychological connections between people and their physical environments. The title of the seminar was hopeful.

It was a hot Saturday afternoon. We sat in rows on black chairs paying partial attention to words from the lectern that never occurred to Wordsworth, Wallace Stevens, Merwin, or Manley Hopkins: Positivistic orientation, Radical empiricism, Hegemonic configuration. My mind wandered. There were no mentions of love, affection, nostalgia. It seemed as though the channels between left and right brains had been effectively blocked by the border guards of reason. I left more than a little disappointed.

The following Saturday I was at the C. G. Jung Institute in San Francisco for our monthly meeting of the Deep River poetry group. A comfortable circle of chairs was arranged on the floral carpet of the library. Through the window a view to a cedar tree taller than the house. We listened attentively to each other's poems—words of love, outrage, amazement, bypassing the rational mind's demand for explanation. Here the psyche was allowed its freedom to soar, explore, pour out its fantasies into the warm receptive hearts of fellow poets.

Those two Saturdays exemplified for me the discomfort I often felt in academia, and the opening to deeper emotions that came through writing poetry. Academic writing demanded research, objectivity, footnotes. Writing poetry encouraged delving into one's heart, reliving memories, expressing startling moments of recognition. I jokingly tell people I am a recovering academic. Studying and writing poetry has been my cure.

Clare Cooper Marcus

For Dylan Thomas

In the dream, I came to you to learn how
to talk to animals.
Now, from the jacket of a book—
your collected poems—your
face stares up at me, quizzical
expression in your eyes,
brown as owls.
Graceful fall of fingers holding
a small cigar.
From your lips words
                    hurtled
                          circled
                                somersaulted
along the sea-shanked shores of Wales.

Into those cupped ears, the sounds of
bells from foggy steeples,
murmurings of ancient stones,
tales told by seagulls in the tide-throbbing
jetties of your mind.
You wrote that you were—
    young and easy
    under the apple boughs
    green and carefree in the lamb–white days
Caught in your questioning gaze I feel
old, moving slowly through the sheep–grey
days of winter.
There are blackbirds carving through
my memories,
thick as solid salt.

Moon–scaled fish rest
in my aging hands, praying for water.
Souls of rabbits I had killed
silent as bones,
wait for me to learn
their lost and lovely language.

Clare Cooper Marcus

Like an Assyrian Hound

I wish I could howl like an Assyrian hound,
be mystical and terrifying
in my grief cries over deepest longings
locked away in rooms at the back
of an old Victorian on Noname Street.

I want to be burning brightly in a Blakean
night, growling, eyes luminous, teeth
glistening white, sharpening my claws
on a tree with leaves of fire, vines of lightning.
Above me, the full moon reflects my blaze.

I want to be a conquistador
from Salamanca, bringing horses
to the New World, riding over a high ridge
with you, to discover a vast ocean,
where we then swim.

I want to be a flying dragon, swooping
down to save you from years of slavery
in Babylon ~ breathing you in, a gentle
maiden; breathing you out, a glowing
ember. I laugh when you complain
about the texture of my tongue.

I want to be a Sultan, ruling from
the Alhambra in Moorish Spain, alone
with you in my throne room. You dance for me
until I give you everything, with gratitude.
And then, you make me howl.

Kent Ward Butzine

Mammal Night

When the full moon comes,
the pace of life quickens
with gravity's gentle tilt.

One after another,
the women arrive
bellies swollen with beings,
labor underway.

My clogs squeak against the smooth, tiled corridor,
rush in, rush out,
water, ice chips, pain medicine, warm blankets,
offer something of comfort if I can
to my mammal sisters
as they growl, and moan,
and shout against the night.

Moments become infinities.
Bodies cleave in two.

Finally,
a baby's first cry,
a sudden awareness
of the wonder of us.

In a single moment,
the blood flowing through a tiny human's lungs reverses,
flows from breath, to lungs, to hummingbird heart.

To greet these new arrivals,
Heavy–light,
Full of moon and places beyond our reach,
This is my work.

Raluca Ioanid

What Science Would Have Me Believe

They say it's a hormone
a neurotransmitter

just another by–product
of the hypothalamus

coursing through the blood stream
causing me to feel this way

however, when I look at this tiny
still wrinkly vernix–covered being

or hear his unbecoming yet
amusing snorting sounds

while valiantly struggling to latch on
to his mother's big brown aching nipples

or hold his perfect little body against my chest
our hearts beating a new song

these feelings are more than an oxytocin–high
and these glistening tears sliding down my cheeks

are nothing less than
liquid prayers of gratitude

Anita Cadena Sánchez

The Ship

Dear God, please turn the ship
that floats in the rain above Foothill Blvd
It lands in an apple orchard
My back merges with the land

Dear God the land has got my back
The apple trees are blooming
It snows in the foothills
Apple blossoms fall on my grave

Dear God, my heart overflows with rain
It snows apple blossoms in the desert
The ship is climbing Mount Qaf
I am drowning

Dear God please help me catch my plane
on top of the mountain
A mystic stays dry in the sea
The sea is full of roses

Dear God it's raining rose petals at home
My car is bleeding on a dusty road
The ship sails along the meridian
Rain yearns for the sea

Daniela Kantorová

Nine crows in my backyard

perch
on tall viridian cypress.
Drought claims our golden nubs,
the Sierra foothills.
Brown bleeds through any promise
of first–green blades
from sole autumn downpour.

When a Pineapple Express
blasts through—
feathers plaster,
roots swell,
clouds scurry toward the plains.
And still the birds fly by
or sway high on the row of towering trees.

At last with our tropical–gale winds long
                                          gone,
not a speck of dust anywhere,
out of a blue–glass sky
flapping and squawking the crows
en masse land.

On black stilt legs, each bird
a pumpjack—glistening, stabbing
through lush grass,
California's winter cloak.
They hunt and peck, shift
around their murder's center.

The bounty,
worms rise
above the soaked sable soil
while the crows
eat
and
eat.

Sheila deShields

The Swim

I'm 33.3 years old
have sworn off weed,
wine, cigarettes,
my manic hippie boyfriend—
a man who could set
a clock to pleasure—
I watch him drive off
in his one-eyed Ford
and I wail with no relief.

28 days later, to cheer me up
Jill & Laura road trip it
from Appalachia to Puget Sound.
We ride the ferry to Orcas Island:
rocky shores, clouds,
sunlit emerald waves.

On my friend Ron's land
our sleeping bags lie
under July's evening sun.
It's that fallow time of day.
Jill grabs a beer from the cooler,
Laura rolls a joint on a magazine,
passes it over to me.

The yes-no war in my head
cease-fires when Ron's girlfriend,
Tracy—a sturdy spitfire—
bids from her Honda Accord
"Anyone want to go for a swim?"

I follow her down a path
wrecked by blackberry bushes
picked clean. At the edge
of a shady lagoon—
a jagged floating jungle
of fallen cedars—
we drop our clothes, slide in.

Tracy swims ahead, then
points skyward,
"*Osprey!*" she says
in a séance whisper.
3 seconds later
and a breaststroke in front of me
the winged raptor—
with its brown-feathered cape
& broad white belly—
thrashes her legs
to skewer a salmon the size of my forearm
with her knife-sharp talons.

The sobering kill, an elixir:
I keep swimming
into the furthest corner
where a bald eagle stands
on a log. She sees me,
bends forward and drinks
from the dark water,
then circles up to the light.

Connie Hills

69

Leopard

The dreamer looks down
On a writhing mass
Zooms in for a closer look
Sees a leopard fooling around
Playing like a kitten
Its four supple spotted legs
Its head spotted too
But the body is black like a dark room
With all the doors closed
There is an absence of light
Its sleek ears are black too
This animal didn't come from a zoo

The dreamer spots two human cubs
Showing no sense of fear
Of the hybrid leopard
Who writhes so near
They are unaware
Imaginary animals
Have their own way
To devour their prey

The watcher keeps her distance

Maybe it's really a love cat
Who found a pair of playmates
Come to enjoy their time out of the cage

Virginia Lee Chen

Coming, Going

pulsing like the breath, the flow
of atmosphere through the body's pump, the slow
transformation from red to bruisy blue,
the day, the night, the in, the out, the little river
hunts down the hill, cutting her way
through mud and gravel, dislodging
trunks, uprooting boulders, never looks back
till she leaps the cliff to meet the sandy tide.

I would love to crash like waves,
splinter light, fracture bedrock,
      break down
into mist and get called up by the sun,
travel in the continuous flow between
constant cold night at the bottom of the deep
and playing in the surf with pail and shovel.

Let's build a fort with crenelations
      towers and turrets, sand and water:
we'll dig till the tide sweeps our castles away.

To come and to go in the terror of birth,
naked and squalling, years to recoup:

stack stone on mortar:
raise a tower, build a self,
      till the wind chews off the corners
      till the tide digs out the foundations
      till the moon tugs off the crown...
          everything eventually must fall down.

We are not designed to let go
easily, we build ourselves on skeletons
as an argument against flow...

unless we study the redwood who rises
ring by century impossibly high
to spit mist into a mountain landscape captured
        by a swift sable brush.

                                        Dossie Easton

A Hard Price

a rock—Oklahoma Hackett, part mossy, half-buried
crusted in red-brown dirt

a tractor—John Deere near-rolling-over, turning rows
driven by a sweat-soaked farmer-rancher, hanging on

children—a girl, seven, and the other twelve, near-a-man
grimy faced, gloves no-fingers-left, grasping stones

a wheelbarrow—rusted, weighted by rock after rock
each trip on one wobbling bald tire

an accumulating heap—heated up, hours inching by
a burden to be moved onto a beaten-up Ford truck

a mound of loads—half the height of a pumpjack
set forty years later in the middle of that 80 acres

at the end of a line of oil wells
which will

putter   out
we were given

a fought-for meadow by end of summer earned
swaying golden prairie grasses, Bermuda and vetch
a herd of grazers
sweet Herefords, pink-eye-free Angus, and later
                                    towering Texas longhorns
a business of stone 30 years down that dirt road,
its rock from the meadow and five Midwest states

the grassland—
enough

the oil rig—
enough

again and again
the ground survives

Sheila deShields

IV

The symbol is the word...that rises out of the depths of the self...and places itself unexpectedly on the tongue...as though a door opens leading into a new room...

C.G. Jung[18]

---

[18] *The Red Book,* p. 311.

A Way to Love

There is an elusive feel to what we call *soul*. In writing poetry, I am able to spread out into this feeling, embody it best I can with words. Often this comes by way of an encounter that has touched me deeply, changed me, connected me to the numinous, or slid me into the continuation of consciousness. The shadow—or duende—is the place where the grit, fecundity, and vitality of such an experience connects us all. Reading and writing poetry is a way for us to unify when we are adrift from our core of love. Poetry is a way back to love.

Connie Hills

God of Garbage

The tall muscular Jamaican
jumps down from a garbage truck.
He unlocks our Ivy St.
alley door,
pushes it forward, hops inside.
He pivots his torso and legs,
then high jumps—
one arm stretching straight up
to trip a lever. Magic.
The main garage door rolls open.

Soon—drum rolling
fifty-pound black trash bins—
he's singing *"Little darlin', stir it up
Come on and stir it up."*

Each Christmas,
I baked butter cookies
before dawn, waited
for the hydraulic
brake horns
signaling his arrival.

Remover of filth, ferment,
everything that is dying.

In my paisley bathrobe
I hurried that parcel
into his hands, thanked him.

His smile, like heliotrope
in warm bloom,
a braid of sea otters
swimming the tide,
merriment in a cataclysm,
cinnamon swirls of time.
I could have loved him.

Connie Hills

After the Dharma Talk

And the miraculous comes so close...
not known to anyone at all,
but wild in our breast for centuries.
                    Anna Akhmatova[19]

I walked quietly back to my cabin
that night after Norman's Dharma Talk
in the Zendo at Tassajara.
I didn't feel like talking.
When I sat down to take off my sandals,
I started to cry. Not sure why.

In my mind was the Akhmatova poem,
especially the part about what's wild
in our breasts, that we don't know at all,
that keeps us from complete despair.

There's a line in a song that was popular
in the 1970s, called "Werewolves
of London," by Warren Zevon, now
deceased. The line, that's been sifting
through me, is —"He's that hairy-handed
gent / who ran amok in Kent," and
my association, my question, since
my name is Kent, is—when am **I**
going to feel this wild, hairy thing
running amok **in me**?!

---

[19] from *Poems of Akhmatova,* p. 73, selected, translated, and
introduced by Stanley Kunitz with Max Hayward (Little, Brown
and Co).

Sorry about the self-focus, but that
is the focus—the fabricated self-
structure, with its fictions, blockages
and shields, growing in the fertile soil
of family conflict, turmoil, and terror.

"Why did you do that?" my father shouted.
"I don't know," my child self answered,
shaking. "You **have to know!** There's
a reason for everything."

On a "fix-up" date, sitting next to her
at the concert, I'm enclosed, frozen over.
Maybe she too; I couldn't know, couldn't feel.

Oh, to be unbounded!
To scream, to stomp, to smear—
To dance, roar, fuck, paint, sing

> *Aw - ooo*
> *Aw - ooo*
> *Werewolves of London*
> *Aw – ooo*

Sing it with me!

> *He's that hairy handed gent*
> *who ran amok in Kent*
> *Aw - ooo*
> *Werewolves of London*
> *Aw – ooo*

Kent Ward Butzine

Pan Korikian
Delphi

Beside an ancient juniper
high up on Parnassus
far from any oracle
a great cavern opens
        vagina to the Planet.

Dripping granite, mossy pillars,
rippling curtains petrify.
The children of the mountain
do not speak the future:
They open the Earth to the Sky.

Rumor has it Pan nests here.

Mighty Goat–foot, Your great Cock
has eyes that see the dark,
deep down where Desire pulses
red and warming You spurt dreams
deep into our Mother:
Earth quakes to meet Your Gaze.

Down in the dark where Persephone ripens,
Gaea composts our slow burning resentments
our squirming fears: So Spring arises
    from Winter's dying ambition.

If Pan should come to open me,
stretch me around His thick wild Vision,
shred all my costumes
        with His bright sharp Horns:
His Cock's Eyes see only naked truth.

Lover of Earth, Your bright Cock
rips up history, then You
shake us awake to rebuild
        what You have torn apart;
and we will erect another history
for You to destroy again...

Dance on my grave, Goat–foot,
Welcome me home. I will ride
Your huge Laugh deep inside our Mother,
deeper and darker,
till Your Cock's Eyes
Light elsewhere.

                    Dossie Easton

Ghazal of the Boy in My Dream

After gumbo and jazz   after rain on my head   you befell me
                                                 in a dream
Strange boy   your spiraling hands   your eyes ablaze   cast a spell
                                                 in my dream

Worlds are created by alphabet   Take Seven Hebrew letters
                                                 Seven chakras
Deep breath   Add tincture of heaven and hell   I make poems
                                                 in your dream

It's been ten years since Katrina   Say "Lower Ninth" and weep
                                                 Say House of Blues
and I'm singing   that old time conch shell refrain   me and the boy
                                                 in my dream

How long have you lived in my heart child   alphabet balm
                                                 for sorrow and ache?
You open the doors to The Mysteries   compel me to enter
                                                 by way of the dream

There's food for the soul   in image   in word   in down beat and
                                                 in the blues
                                                 There's a place
I know   without hunger or thirst   where spirit and maker dwell
                         Some call it a poem   Some call it a dream

The pedicab sprite plays the sax   and dances the second line
                                                 He transports me back
a lifetime ago   to a rickshaw careening through India
        Call him Ariel   call him Ishmael   Who am I in his dream?

84

Words send their roots to the bottom of time and I   your alphabet dowser
                                                                    feel the tug
of your poems   Dig deep the well Naomi   draw me a bucket
                         of olden rains   to water the word   in your dreams

Naomi Ruth Lowinsky

You Tell Me You Never Forget

that you are Black. Constant
flowing streams of shocks echo and eddy,
constantly alert:

See this small child puzzled
          in the playground.
See this tall boy not playing
basketball. See this musician
playing Go.

What is it like to see your face
distorted in the mirror of every other face
passing in the street? You told me
you can hear the click of car doors
locking when you wait to cross Laguna Street
          to the Zen Center:

In the market in the country town
where I live, a stranger asked you
if you were lost.

You can never forget that you are Black
so I am trying to remember that I am white.

                              Dossie Easton

Ambivalence is...

when words fail to materialize
when you find you must wear a larger pant size
when you sing a song but you have the lyrics all wrong
when you can't recall why you chose to write this poem at all

ignoring those hobgoblins of the little mind even as
you write the same line 500 times without dotting an *i* or crossing a *t*
but you shrug it off to tell yourself   well some days go that way

Ambivalence peeks at you from the other side of the mirror
sees those eyebrows turning white and stray whiskers around the lips
                                                          & chin
Ambivalence smiles to herself as she calls your bluff
knowing you'll rise to the challenge
write and strut your stuff

                                        Anita Cadena Sánchez

Genus of Weeds

In the books they call them volunteers.
Neither drafted nor recruited,
an army of weeds marches in to battle barrenness.
Smuggled in by squirrels and possums,
Wayward blossoms, eager, hopeful
sling seeds promiscuously
and send out shoots
for the advancing forest. Most of them
cannot be found in field guides: a mysterious identity
is essential to the wisdom of weeds.

Were they exiled from their families
for refusing to get in line, out of order outlaws
who persist in sending runners
wherever the sweet water flows?

No one ever planned to cultivate me.
My parents had pictured a more faintly
blushing rose, coaxed into bloom
            in a bud vase.

I grew hardy fighting cultivation,
broke out of their well-tended plot:
cast my self on a whim and a breeze
to seek the eerie bloom of dangerous fruit
and set my roots down in a sanctuary
            for my own wild life

                                        Dossie Easton

Healing the Wound

Between the marigolds and the
purple sprouting broccoli
a plastic garden chair
faded by the sun
folds its arms around my
aging body until I become
Cleopatra on her golden throne

At my feet
between ancient stones
no papyri but
spearmint   wild garlic
drawn from dark depths
by the daily passage of the
sun-god
Ra

First gardens
aided by the flooding of the Nile
mine is the creation of my hands
and passing clouds of time
microbes and the rain
earthworms   black–backed beetles
and the blessing of the sun
now   a safe place away
from virus and death
lurking beyond
its borders
Not far from where I sit
birds visit a feeder   no sacred ibis but
black–capped chickadee
towhee   warbler   robin   blue jay

I freeze   they do not see me
eyes closed I recall a dream
black bird with white beak
nestles against my thigh
to heal the wound
brought by the surgeon's
knife
it is a coot
exploring the unconscious
to retrieve sustenance for life
diving the waters
of the Nile
algae and mollusks morphing
to messages of resurrection

Clare Cooper Marcus

Pandémie Hypnagogique

Everything is receding   darkening
there is sadness   as the trees go
the river   birds and birdsong   the sky
all beloved

I can't write   I can paint a little
but I can't write

who will tell my story?   should I care?
what is   am *I*?
and how to tell the story?

perhaps my paintings   my music playlists
my bills   pretty much paid up
all the messes I couldn't keep up with
the things I wrote about   when I could

perhaps there will be   some kind of dawning
but if not it will be okay

no regrets
a letting be

you
have made this possible

dancing to the blues
we hear BB King with his Lucille sing

I've got a sweet little angel
I love the way she spreads her wings
when she spreads her wings around me
I get joy and everything

                              Kent Ward Butzine

Flight of the Mind

in memory of Ursula Kroeber LeGuin (1929 – 2018)

i.

if the world turns empty
and i am the glass holding nothin'
nothin' at all

i won't remember my beloved Granny
stroking my head in her lap
listening as I tell her story's end

i won't have a memory of Grandpa with his level
teaching me to find a horizontal plane
my lesson and my grandfather   lost   lost

ii.

i have seen elders growing   old
as their universe collapses into dementia
until we are on top of one another

like monuments
stacked
on a single parcel of barren ground

when i escort my mother's neighbor from the elevator
she asks   *do you live here   wanna go shopping*
and she disappears into a stranger's room   hers   hers

iii.

in my last days
may i sit by the black basalt fountain   wild blue
    irises
and hooded orioles among my redwood trees

let me recall the names of my children
while a long–tailed marsh wren
scurries in dark dirt under my magenta geranium

let me have sturdy steps next to my granddaughter
and like LeGuin
listen to the high-hummed hummingbird

may i welcome old friends in my last green garden
hear voices of others while speaking my own
fierce as sparrowhawks   aware   aware

Sheila deShields

Spring's Catch

incandescent flowers   white
sweet-scented candles
of the California buckeye[20]

beneath
horse chestnuts   glossy mahogany like the eyes of a deer
last year's poison

when ground down
scattered on streams   a Pomo powder
stunning fish   easily–captured

if leached like acorns
a sustaining flour

bane or bounty
in silence

spiked glory
rooted to blaze

longlived
like words   breathing

Sheila DeShields

---

[20] An endemic species, the California buckeye has an estimated lifespan of
nearly 300 years.

V

*I am weary my soul, my wandering has lasted
too long, my search for myself outside of myself...
I found you when I least expected you. You climbed
out of a dark shaft. You announced yourself...
in dreams.*

C.G. Jung[21]

---

[21] *The Red Book*, p. 233.

V

How Poems Come and What They Can Bring

The experience of an assisting force coming from somewhere outside ourselves is nearly universal among practicing artists. We can be slowly, painfully trudging along with the intention to create when suddenly the words begin to flow easily, effortlessly, as though we've become a channel for something beyond ourselves, wiser and clearer than ourselves, an unanticipated gift which sooner or later departs as suddenly as it arrived. As Vincent van Gogh, in a letter to a friend, wrote, "art is something which, although produced by human hands, is not created by human hands alone, but something which wells up from a deeper source in our souls."[22]

Since ancient times, this experience has given rise to the sense, or construct, of the Muse. (Homer's *The Odyssey* begins with the words, "Sing in me, Muse, and through me tell the story . . .) This figure of great blessings and mysteries is the primary focus of my poem, "The Vow," (see page 100) which portrays the essential nature of the Muse, how she (or he) can be invoked, what she brings to a poem, what is asked in return, and how her gifts can most readily be received and integrated. I wrote this poem five or six years ago, don't remember much about what went into its composition, and don't have the sense of it being *my* poem. Instead I find it intriguing to reflect upon, as though it comes from another realm.

The Muse can bring truly precious gifts, but she does ask something in return. As a precondition, actually, for her presence, she asks for a commitment, a vow. The ritual context of this vow—the Muse bringing something of herself, almost a part of herself, to be signed, the poet dipping his quill into "liquid night" and signing without hesitation or conceptual understanding—indicates that this is no ordinary, daytime contract, with fine print and lawyers present. Rather, it involves the

---

[22] *The Complete Letters of Vincent van Gogh*, Volume 3, pp. 399-400 (Thames and Hudson).

signature of the heart, a commitment of the soul, a recognition and honoring of what matters most. Consistency of practice, broadly defined, will be the determining factor for the presence of the Muse. Sculptor Richard Serra's statement that "work comes out of work"[23] is another way of saying this. In any case, the Muse will not be following a prescribed schedule; she will come when she decides the time is right.

The Muse is both a part of oneself and a part of the natural world, a part that is "wild" and cannot be controlled. Actually, very little can be controlled by our individual egos. Recognizing this, and taking it in, can become another immensely valuable gift from the Muse. It can become a source of great relief.

Waiting in darkness. This is a foundational practice of a poet, or any artist. There are significant periods of time when nothing, or nothing satisfactory, comes, from the Muse or from anywhere else. John Keats[24] counseled the development of Negative Capability, by which he meant "capable of being in uncertainties, mysteries, doubts, without any irritable reaching after fact and reason." This capacity can be facilitated, at least for some, through regular meditation practice, where everything that comes is welcomed or, when not, the unwelcoming is welcomed.

Here is Rainer Maria Rilke's[25] advice, from *Letters to a Young Poet*, about waiting in darkness: "Being an artist means: not numbering and counting, but ripening like a tree, which doesn't force its sap, and stands confidently in the storms of spring, not afraid that afterwards summer may not come. It does come. But it comes only to those who are patient, who are there as if eternity lay before them, so unconcernedly silent

---

[23] Serra, Richard, *Drawings—Work Comes Out of Work*, (Kunsthaus Bregenz—front cover). See also—Richard Serra, Gargosian Gallery: gargosian.com/artists/richard-serra/

[24] Keats, John, *The Complete Poetical Works and Letters of John Keats*, Cambridge Edition, p. 277 (Houghton, Mifflin and Co).

[25] Rilke, Rainer Maria, *Letters to a Young Poet, pp. 24-25, translated by Stephen Mitchell (Vintage Books).*

and vast. I learn it every day of my life, learn it with pain I am grateful for: patience is everything!"

One of the greatest gifts of the Muse, and of Poetry, is in their capacity to help us see more clearly who we really are, and what matters most to us. Jane Hirshfield,[26] in her essay on the 17th Century Japanese haiku master, Matsuo Basho, writes: "Basho set forth a simple, deeply useful reminder—that if you see for yourself, hear for yourself, and enter deeply enough into this seeing and hearing, all things will speak with and through you." *All things will speak with and through you!* In other words, the entire world can become our Muse.

I'll end this essay with a final note on the Gifts of Poetry. While teaching at NYU, Galway Kinnell[27] was overheard telling a student, "There is no work on the poem that is not also work on the poet." What a blessed bargain!

May the Muse be with you!

Kent Ward Butzine

---

[26] Hirshfield, Jane, *Ten Windows: How Great Poems Transform the World*, p. 51 (Alfred A. Knopf).

[27] Lentine, Genine, A tribute to Galway Kinnell in honor of his retiring from New York University (2004). (www.geninelentine.com/2014/10/30/galway-kinnell/

The Vow

Dancing through mist, a rising moon
Hiding, flirting among half–illumined
Clouds of night, light skin and
Smiling eyes fleetingly visible
Inside long hair and
Loose–fitting gown,
Whirl of orange and amber.

Stopping by my side, she puts before me
A piece of fabric, the same
Golden–orange cloth as her gown,
Its textures and myriad threads
Now more visible.

"Sign this," she says.

With neither hesitation nor
Understanding, I dip my feather quill
Into liquid night
And sign with a flourish.

Then she is off, moving quickly
To the haunting melody she sings,
Holding in her left hand the fabric
That carries my mark, a seed
Precariously dancing at the edge
Of an empty field.

With my body, my senses,
I follow my soul as best I can
Toward fading flashes of light

A destiny
Fully determined,
Totally unknown.

Waiting in darkness

Ready to be held
Ready to be taken

Kent Ward Butzine

Old Song

When I was me I remembered[28]
The songs of the stars
Before I was born

When I was me I remembered
The smell of the ages
Before the fall

When I was me I remembered
The silence of the sky
Before the birds sang

When I was me I remembered
The sounds of the earth
The seasons never heard

When I was me I remembered
I once was me

Before the dog barked
Before the door closed
Before the black bird came

Virginia Lee Chen

---

[28] This line is from W.S. Merwin's poem "Natural History of Forgetting," in *The Moon Before Morning*, p. 109, (Copper Canyon).

poem for Lucille Clifton

here's another bone to pick with you
o mother whose bones i worry for scraps

you
      asked me to carry you on my back
      when i crossed the atlantic out of my teens into
                               womanhood
      used your degree in Jungian counseling
      to demand that i explain myself
      thought you'd thrown a replica pot
      when i was born a girl   a bona fide made–in–the–USA
                               boomerang

but i
      herded cattle on a horse without a saddle   got
                     thrown   and picked myself up
      dreamed a gossamer sail and stitched it to my
                     mid back   bloodied and torn
      delved into other countries of sin and glories
      found my wilderness within and satellite
                     constellations above
      scrubbed my own floors
      dug my hands into red dirt to grow herbs   a
                     husband   and sons
      lit a candle to find my way home
      pounded my heart into words to breathe

                        Sheila deShields

Way Finding

Here at the planet's half way point
there is majesty at every turn
my gaze becomes new.

Just outside of Otavalo,
at the edge of town past the railroad tracks,
Peguche falls roars down from the mountain,
mist envelopes me,
the water's wild rush shatters
a stuckness within.

In the cloud forest
the thick canopy churns with life-force,
afternoon downpours drench
but never silence
tree songs and bird orchestras

The furl and unfurl of wings.
Expansion contraction.
The hummingbird's hearts beating 1,200 beats per minute.
zipping from flower to flower, barely touching long enough to sip
sweet nectar.

My mind can be the same, zipping from thought to thought,
fear to fear, crisis to crisis,
not stopping to drink in the breath, the moment.
These tiny, fervent birds in their nonstop flight teach me again to
breathe.

In the Andes,
light steps over many miles,
a kaleidoscope of greens
teach me again the gift of walking in peace,
present moment, wonderful moment.

Every breath,
even the desperate gulps for oxygen at 11,000 feet
a chance for joy,
an opportunity for arriving,
here, now.

The Earth gives me comfort.
I remember the strength of my gait.
May her abundant, fertile, magical force
teach me the abundance in me, too.

Raluca Ioanid

Grace

to W.S. Merwin

where the running path curves
in the unmade light of fog
i can see the feral orchard
long left to fend for itself

between the path and the fence
a single drooping fruit hangs
like an egg unharvested
its tether unknown in the swirling damp

i stare at the tiny lime green kernel
hard and tight
centimeters from my face
and then see others dangling

drupes overhead by the hundreds
their exposed ripening
their trusting the light to come
in this   our pandemic   season

i might have stood in orchards forever
and not brushed against hidden colors
or not have awakened to a newfound
                                    abundance
as i neared

and i might have forgotten my apricot jam
soft gold fruit picked from the abandoned
                                    orchard
across the street
from our first house

or not remembered the heady honeyed juice
on my fingers
on a crust of porridge bread
on your lips

what if i had forgotten the taste of your mouth
on a gray morning
when i feared our ill child would never run
among the breathing trees

                              Sheila deSheieds

Pacific Ode

I arrived at twenty one with two duffel bags and a box of books
to the land of adult runaways, before the tech boom,
home of the poets, the dancers, the muralistas,
free spirits and social justice fighters.

This landscape held my hope and determination
in its giant hand, and taught me how to be.
Standing on the ridge of Point Reyes,
where two tectonic plates drift in opposition to birth the ever
widening Tomales Bay,
I finally shed my city skin.

At Baker Beach
I submerged myself again and again
into the Pacific's wild slippery coldness,
wishing for rebirth.

Over the years the sand hugged my curves,
embraced my lovers,
the wet salt lick of coastal
fog on our tender flesh.

The ocean fed us glistening oysters,
salmon hearts,
Dungeness crabs
pulled from metal traps with our bare hands.

Eventually, I gained mastery over the continent's curling edge,
Lands End and the burnt red of the Golden Gate Bridge
That I'd often thought to jump from

I learned to ride my bike further and further,
from the densely packed Mission
through the Panhandle and out past the Presidio,
eventually to Marin, guided by spring poppies
arching hopeful orange heads towards sunshine
down into the fertile wetness under the Redwood trees
up and over Mount Tamalpais.

It's been seventeen years,
And now I'm headed towards the Blue Ridge Mountains,
with the contents of a full house, a life full,
a husband and a cat,
the Pacific etched into my heart.

Raluca Ioanid

California

California, you have entered me
as a home away from home
migration after migration,
as a new life
When I took a cab in London to Heathrow
the song that played as we drove down the embankment was
Beautiful Day

California, you have woven yourself into me
and under my skin
the ancient energy of redwood trees
I claimed
I could drive the Tioga road with my eyes closed

California, you have lured me in
The misty views of Nepenthe
The glass of wine I will fess up to
The Ocean was benevolent to us both

California, you have entered my core
when I saw the blood in your streets
and an old man told me:
"There is an underground here and it will protect you"

California, you have given birth to me
An African woman, houseless, said:
"I can see in your eyes you're not a civilian"

California, you have haunted my spirit
when I played dominoes one day on a windy

Vallejo waterfront
I can never forget

California, you have devoured me
I am digesting you

Daniela Kantorová

In a Dark Season

When the dreary cold of winter comes
I want to be a bear
I want to go deep into the earth
to a lair with visions
painted on the walls

I want to slow down
and down
down to the faintest
rhythm of life
to the slow slow blues
of the heart

I want to be content
with the darkness
the stillness
the solitude
with time away
in the cycle of the seasons

A time of non-doing
a time perhaps
for dreaming the ancient dreams
of cavern journeys
and river crossings
with sacred companions
to reach the underworld
that place where darkness is
celebrated
as fully
as the coming
of first
light

Kent Ward Butzine

Birth Day Poem 2017

Carry me back   through the laboring dark
into first light   first cry   first touch
of mother's hands   Those hands

broad palmed   big fingered   always working
kitchen hands   comfort hands   hands that tried
to stitch the world back together

when father erupted   the furies took over
It was the summer of '43   What did they know
my young parents   about the Europe they'd fled

the trains   the chimneys   What happened
to Father's mother   his father   his sister Maia   named
for that goddess who dances with veils   Some say

She's illusion   Some say She's creation
plays with imagination   Then rips
the magic carpet away

Carry me back to that cave   I clambered into
decades ago   hushed by the resonant dark
where ancient hands shaped   Her stony vagina   just so

at noon   on the Vernal Equinox   a ray of sun
would penetrate   Her innermost   Look
through the rocky lips of Her vulva   the earth

bears fruit   Your little life   and mine   in the flow
of all the mothers of mothers   the grandmothers of magic
the daughters of ritual skill   who carry us   living and dead

Come   Sit with me by the fire   though bones ache
memory flickers   hands lose their hold
on the world   Those evil spirits   who spooked

my cradle   are back   The fire spits
and sputters   The furies   rave
and mutter   Here comes Maia

dancing in the flames   She who lit
the fire   of every life I've lived
has no patience   with lamentation   Shows me

her teeth   and I know   it is She
who will carry me out   through the laboring dark
when it's time   She

who will rip
the veils

Until then   I gather my harvest
love   laughter   dreams   poems
This one's for Her

                              Naomi Ruth Lowinsky

The Solace of Silence in a Chattering World

Silence between the curtains
and the splattered glass
silences sleeping between paragraphs
zendo silence after
the bell has sung
silences of arcing gulls
their mewing cries eaten
by the insistent wind
silences between silvery lines
of new dug furrows in a fallow field
between the petals of a newly opened flower
the silence between fence posts
strung with barbed wire
whose shadows cast a melody of semiquavers
no one hears
red–pillowed rocks which hissed and steamed
and then
fell silent for a billion patient years
the silence between lightning flash
and thunder crash
the silence of the world calling forth its name
silence after the last out breath
when the next in–breath
never comes
the silence between the question
"Do you love me?"
before the answer comes

Clare Cooper Marcus

CONTRIBUTORS

Kent Ward Butzine, Ph.D., is a licensed clinical psychologist and college professor, now retired. He lives with his life–partner in the San Francisco Bay Area. Painting and drawing have been joyous activities for him since childhood, but only since retirement has some degree of consistent practice become possible. Poetry, both reading and writing, is a newer love, which has grown exponentially since joining Deep River over 12 years ago. The group's facilitator, Naomi Lowinsky, and fellow participants, have created a safe, comfortable, nurturing environment for the exploration and celebration of poetry and its many gifts. Kent says that "Naomi is the embodiment of wisdom and compassion. She, and the delightful, generous, skillful group members, have expanded my horizons and deepened my soul in terms of both poetry and life, which have become one. At times, I now actually think of myself as a poet. That would not have been possible without Deep River."

Virginia Lee Chen has a PhD in Mythological Studies from Pacifica Graduate Institute. She began writing her dissertation on Orpheus while on a journey to Antarctica. On the way, she traveled with an unlucky couple. The husband failed to save his wife from falling off a cliff. Following that, Virginia lost four loved ones in four years. The inner work of poetry with Naomi Lowinsky and the Deep River poets helped her to survive the grief.

A mezzo-soprano, she sang with the San Francisco Opera, Carmel Bach Festival, and Philharmonia Baroque Orchestra. She received a fellowship to the Bach Aria Festival and Institute at Stony Brook.

Virginia was born and raised on a ranch in California where she spent the weekends riding her retired race horse, Echo. Her mother called the mare an "old nag." Even so, she sang all the songs she knew to Echo as she rode through the countryside. She loves jazz.

117

Sheila deShields balances with one foot on a ranch in Oklahoma and one foot in the Bay Area of CA. Interviewed on National Public Radio for her essay "Sunset Tales," published in *At Grandmother's Table*, she has poems published in literary magazines and newspapers such as *Comstock Review* and *The Halifax Herald*. She is a founding member of Hedgebrook Sisters Writing Group and a recipient of Hedgebrook and Rotary International Fellowships. Deep River compels her to voice vision, joy and concerns louder, please! Lucille Clifton, poet of light, woke her up to speaking more truth. W. S. Merwin showed her a long life committed to our planet, our need to work for love and its unexpected, unearned gifts that ripple into our souls. Naomi brings a cornucopia of poets past and present that speak of times as hard as, or more difficult than, our own. She and her poets grab Sheila by the neck and shake her into gratefulness to try again, to listen, to write.

Dossie Easton, Marriage & Family Therapist, is co-author with Janet W. Hardy of *The Ethical Slut* (now in its 3rd Edition) and four other books about alternative sexualities. In her private practice in San Francisco she works with individuals, couples and moresomes, and it has been her privilege to supervise several interns preparing to serve the often misserved communities of sexual outsiders. Her articles for therapists about alternative sexualities include "Making Friends with Your Jealousy" in *Understanding Non-Monogamies* and "Shadowplay: S/M Journeys to Your Selves" in *Safe, Sane & Consensual*. Her poetry has been published in several topical anthologies. Dossie is creator and lead teacher of the Navigating Consent classes, which you can learn more about at www. navigating-consent.com. Dossie has been a member of the Deep River Poetry Circle for around ten years where she has experienced unlimited inspiration, encouragement and just plain love that have transformed writing poetry from nervous work to unmitigated delight, thanks to our amazing teacher, Naomi Lowinsky. You can find Dossie's website at www.dossieeaston.com.

Connie Hills

Cauldrons of creativity lie hidden in San Francisco.

Once, over the course of five years, in the foggy hollow of Noe Valley, she exchanged juicy poems with a Jungian Analyst. Say, she was branded as a poet.

Fifteen years later—on a Pacific Heights perch—inside the Jung Institute's library, *Deep River* writers exchanged fiery poems with Naomi Lowinsky, also a Jungian Analyst and poet. Jungians are dripping in creativity. For the next five years, Hills bathed in, read out loud, and wrote poems *under the influence* of "The Greats."

Two became her muses: James Baldwin for his sensuality and truth-telling—white people will one day fall down (as we are, today)—and Yusef Komunyakaa for his alchemy—turning his Vietnam terror into poetry.

Along the way, her poems have appeared in *Red Wheelbarrow Literary Magazine, Red Rock Review, Porter Gulch Review, The Bark Magazine, and the 2018-19 San Diego Poetry Annual.*

Raluca Ioanid was born in communist Romania and raised in capitalist New York City. By day she is a UCSF trained Family Nurse Practitioner working at a community health center. By night she is a writer of stories and poems. Her work has been published in several anthologies and literary journals. She feels immensely grateful to share a place among the *Deep River* writers, guided by Naomi on a powerful journey into the heart of poetry. She is nourished and healed by the words of the poets they have studied, most notably: James Baldwin, Sandra Cisneros, Lucille Clifton and Galway Kinnell. Through them and the work of her *Deep River* fellows, Raluca has found strength and light for these dark times.

Daniela Kantorová, PsyD, is Czech Bahá'í clinical psychologist and community organizer living in Oakland, California. She is clinical faculty at the Wright Institute, president of Psychologists for Social Responsibility for 2020, co-chair of the first responders committee of Anti Police–Terror Project, and a coordinator of its mental health crisis response team, MHFirst, in Oakland. She specializes in work with survivors of trauma caused by interpersonal and state violence. Her writing and photography on topics of US police terror, mass incarceration and community responses has been featured in Czech publications Nový prostor, A2larm, Romea and Romano voďi.She has been writing poetry since her childhood, initially as a means of processing traumatic experiences, finding inspiration in mysticism, nature, punk and movements for liberation. She is eternally grateful to Naomi Lowinsky and the Deep River poetry circle for continuously inspiring and encouraging her poetry writing as a spiritual and healing practice.

Naomi Ruth Lowinsky lives at the confluence of the River Psyche and the Deep River of Poetry. She's a Jungian Analyst, and a widely published poet, winner of the Obama Millennial Award and the Blue Light Poetry Prize. Her fifth poetry collection, *Death and His Lorca,* is forthcoming from Blue Light Press.

Lowinsky has brought those two rivers together in Deep River—a poetry writing circle she's been leading in the library of the San Francisco Jung Institute for 15 years. The group began as a way of working with writing as a spiritual practice. That expanded to writing under the influence of great poets. And before she could say "Open Sesame!" those second Saturday afternoon meetings reverberated with passionate, soulful poems written by the participants. Since the shock of the 2016 election the group's writings have deepened in awareness of shadow, terror, and grief. Naomi is grateful for Deep River, her writing and support group in these awful times. She blogs about poetry and life at www.sisterfrombelow.com.

Clare Cooper Marcus retired as a professor in the College of Environmental Design at UC Berkeley and was looking for a way to deepen her consciousness, too long mired in the publish-or-perish demands of academia. She found what she was looking for among fellow Deep River poets. During World War Two as a child she was evacuated to the English countryside and there found solace in nature. It is not surprising she was drawn to the work of poets of nature and the environment—Gary Snyder, W.S. Merwin—and that she also wrote poems related to times of war. Deep River introduced her to poets of color, such as Gwendolyn Brooks; to others she knew little about such as Frank O'Hara; to those who wrote of poetry's craft such as Annie Finch. With Naomi Lowinsky's provocative prompts she was challenged to delve into her heart, relive painful memories, recognize buried connections. Poetry became her salvation.

Anita Cadena Sánchez received her BA in Economics from Pomona College, and 37 years later she decided to pursue a MA in Consciousness Studies with a certificate in Dream Studies from JFK University to balance out the left–brain demands of her work. Five years ago, a dream led her to the SF Jung Institute website where she fortuitously read about and immediately joined the Deep River poetry writing group. She eagerly accepted her Muse's invitation to put pen to paper. When not writing poetry or dream journaling, she and her husband Steve have the pleasure of caring for their baby grandson Colin, born January 2020.

ACKNOWLEDGEMENTS

With gratitude

To the C.G. Jung Institute of San Francisco, which has hosted Deep River for so many years, and to Baruch Gould and Richard Borutta who did the behind–the–scenes work to make the writing circle possible

To Marianne Morgan and Miranda Lindelow, Institute librarians who have allowed Deep River to meet in their sanctuary

To the Deep River poets, present and past, who have enriched the circle with their creativity and soul

To Raluca Ioanid and Clare Marcus, who helped edit this anthology, as well as all the contributors who gave their time, energy and poetry

To my husband, Dan Safran, who has urged me to make a collection of Deep River poems for years, and who helped with the final editing

To the editors of the following literary magazines in which some of these poems first appeared:

Common Ground Review "Ghazal of the Boy in My Dream"
Evening Street Press "Dead Pheasants"
Front Porch "Birth Day Poem 2017"
New Millennium Writings "Why Am I Here?" (honorable mention)
Origins Journal "Medicine Wheel"
riverbabble "The Ship"

CPSIA information can be obtained
at www.ICGtesting.com
Printed in the USA
FSHW011529120421
80376FS